The Relationship Book

A Practical Guide To

Rekindling Love And Partnership In Your

Relationship

Steve Lovell

© 2019

To my wife Rachel who has shown patience, love and true partnership.

To all at Landmark Worldwide

Content

Why This Book?

As I write this the current divorce rate compiled by the UK Office For National Statistics shows that there were 106,959 divorces of opposite-sex couples in 2016, an increase of 5.8% compared with 2015 and unreasonable behaviour remained the most common grounds for couples divorcing. The current overall figure shows that 42% of marriages end in divorce and the average length of marriages was 11.7 years in 2014. These figures are of course only for people filing for divorce and if you factor in the amount of people who separate and don't file for divorce then the figure is far greater. Also surveys have been conducted that show relationships, where people are chronically unhappy and the figure is 14% (how these particular figures are collected I don't know so I can't be totally confident of their validity). Also imagine the above figures being replicated for couples who choose not to marry and then this equates to a lot of dis-function and unhappiness. We have, I'm sure, all experienced difficulties at some point in our life with our partners and talking to many people about their relationships I see a great deal of pain, anguish and confusion and then this can be compounded by not knowing where to turn to for help.

I started to research the available books out there that have been written to help people with their relationships and although there are not nearly as many relationship books as self-help books there are still many to choose from. I began to read them and follow their suggestions and exercises and, came to the conclusion, that the majority of them were overly complex, technical and very unpragmatic in their approach. They also often focused on the symptoms of failing relationships and looked to fix these rather than getting to the source of why relationships aren't working. I wanted to try a different approach and an approach researched within my own relationship and of those I have coached. My commitment is to supply people with tools that they can use that I know really make a difference and have been used by my wife and I to create a fabulous relationship. I also wanted to present these tools in a simple straight forward and uncomplicated way so that there would be nothing in the way of people being immediately in action, having these tools positively impacting their relationships.

I was faced with a dilemma when approaching writing which was; how do I give it enough substance so that people can relate to it as being substantive, relevant, empirically based and therefore give them the confidence to use it to make a difference to their relationships but then balance it with keeping it readable, direct and pragmatic in its approach. When I speak with clients and friends about what is going on in their relationships that have them not work in the way that they desire, what often comes back is, 'it's just so complicated' ,or, 'I'm so confused', or, 'I don't even know where to begin with sorting it out'. Humans have a tendency to make their problems complicated for the simple reason that they then don't have to take full responsibility in working them out. In my experience, the majority of people would sooner read great tomes about diet, lifestyle, self-help and relationships than be in action. If you find yourself thinking or saying that something is complicated, then chances are you are not prepared to take the required actions to get it sorted! I hope that you find this book direct not weighty, simple not complex, pragmatic not theoretical.

I am not a psychologist although I have worked closely with a team of psychologists and I have no formal relationship training. However, I have been coaching people in improving their relationships and have been trained in transformational coaching for over a decade. I am confident that if you really engage with this material and trust using it then you will experience a new empowerment in your relationship and have a way of creating understanding, love and compassion with your partner.

How best to use this book.

I have written this book with a commitment to people experiencing real positive progress in their relationships that will be sustainable. Most of the Chapters are divided into sections: Introduction, Chapter, Actions and Further Reading. The reason for this was that I want you to start using the book immediately and what's required for that is to read the Introduction and Chapter then to take the Actions. You may wish to look at the Further Reading section later. It's not necessary to read the Further Reading section to get results from this book but it will provide you with a greater understanding of why relationships often look the way they do. I urge you to go immediately into the Actions when you have read the Chapter rather than leaving it a few days or longer as this is when progress will show up. The Chapter and the Actions are both correlated in that one without the other won't provide the maximum effect. There is no magic that will happen from you just understanding what isn't working in your relationship. You need to be in action!

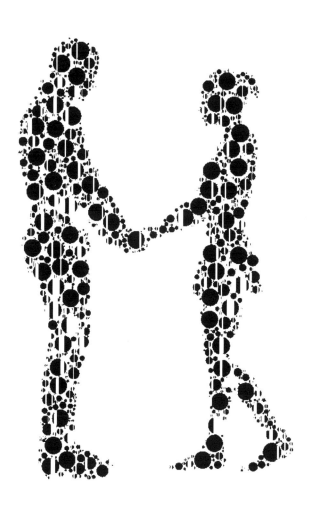

CHAPTER ONE

Talking

Introduction

Most of us remember our first experience of love for our partner. For most of us those early days of a relationship are the most exciting, life affirming, crazy times of our lives, where we have feelings and sensations that occur to us as out of our control and exhilarating. They connect us to our primal nature and take us back to our younger days, when life was for living, not for analysing, worrying and ruminating over. That's when we see the person that we love as a near perfect being and our days are consumed by thoughts of them.

This is how a relationship often unfolds and if this isn't exactly how it went or goes for you then perhaps you can see that you have experienced a version of this. After some time that quirky cute behaviour exhibited by them, that at first occurred as endearing, may now grate like fingernails scraped down a blackboard and those declarations of undying love and lofty plans for the future, are long forgotten, in the daily humdrum of life. OK maybe this is a little overstated for some, but we are often aware that the fun and joy and sometimes love for our partner has dwindled or sometimes completely disappeared. In that first period of love and connection, the way we communicate which was originally from love and commitment may now have eroded into reactionary point scoring. The problem often is that how we were being with our partner and how they were with us is now lost and as much as we may try, we fail to reconnect and get the relationship we had dreamed of back. They just don't seem to be the person that they were.

Contained in this book are some ideas/techniques that I know have worked for couples I have worked with and have worked in my relationship with my wife. No written material can replace what I can offer with personal coaching but, if you and your partner are prepared to draw a line and say 'enough' to how it has been between you and you are now willing to embrace a new approach, then I am confident that this book will make a huge difference to your relationship, whether you feel that the relationship has hit the rocks or you just want to bring some joy and excitement back into it. There are reasons for the order to the different chapters presented here, however there is no advantage to be had from sticking slavishly to the order that I have presented them. You may need to jump backwards or forwards through the Chapters depending on your assessment of how it's going. For instance, if you hit a wall or are struggling with one area of your relationship then you will almost certainly find that one or more of the chapters actions has not been fully completed, or, that maybe it just needs re visiting to give a boost to that area. I request however that Chapter 1 is always completed first. The reason for this will become apparent.

The most effective way of having this material positively impact your relationship is for you and your partner to work together. However, it is possible and not advisable to make a difference to the relationship if it's just you that takes responsibility for having it work. I know that this may occur to you as counter intuitive, as you may be thinking, 'the problem is with them not me', or 'well it takes two to tango', and I address this in later chapters but for now just trust me when I say that you alone can cause a massively positive impact on your relationship, even if your partner is reluctant to do so.

This book is formatted so you can get in action almost immediately. There are exercises to complete at the end of each chapter and then additional reading after that which will assist you in a greater understanding of how we are as humans in relationships. If you just read this book without doing the exercises, then there will be little progress. Action is required!

Getting In Communication

No matter how long you have been together there will be a lot of conversations or interactions with your partner that haven't gone the way you would have liked. There will be things about the relationship that don't work for either of you and haven't worked for some time and you have maybe wanted to address but have been stopped. So, what stops us from communicating openly with our partner? Well it's generally one of the below:

a) We are resigned about the difference that it will make, we have the thought 'well it's pointless saying it again because she/he just doesn't listen to me'. Or 'it's gone too far now to make any difference'

b) 'They always take offense no matter what I say or how I put it.'

c) 'I just don't know where to start or when to say it.'

d) 'I'm scared of their reaction. Maybe they will think that I don't love them anymore.'

e) 'Why should it be me who is always clearing up the mess!'

f) 'Why do I need to say it? It's so obvious that what they are doing is plain wrong! If they don't get that, then there is no hope for us.'

g) Or maybe you are just one of the nice ones who say 'who am I to be saying anything about them and us', but then you go about your day busily complaining about your partner to yourself and probably anyone else who will listen.

h) You say 'well we're not doing that bad, I know of couples who are doing a lot worse and anyway it can never be perfect'

Where we once communicated so openly or, at least thought that we did, we are now shut down and resentful of our partner. The other danger is that our communication and commitment to each other slips away so gradually that we barely notice it. We start out in the relationship having open meaningful conversations, let's generously call that 100% communication, then things happen in the relationship that aren't addressed or, you have arguments that aren't resolved and the communication slips to an 80% but we think that it's still at 100% and then it's slips to let's say 60%. We know at this stage that it's not going well but we still think that we are probably at 80%. After a while the way we communicate with each other has slipped so far but it just appears to us as normal. The way we are with each other is intolerant, righteous, dominating, uncaring and we aren't even present to it! It's just become the way that we communicate and if we had talked to each other in this way at the beginning of the relationship then it wouldn't have even lasted a week! If you can see this at all for yourself then you must get how dysfunctional it has all become when there are two of you operating like this.

How then do we start to move forward? It is essential that before anything new can be generated we need to be in communication where we haven't been in communication previously. I'll use an analogy here to demonstrate. Imagine an outdoor swimming pool that has gathered leaves over the Autumn. If another leaf drops in, then it's no big deal. It will go unnoticed as it will be almost impossible to see amongst all of the other leaves. That's how it's probably been going in your relationship. As I said before it's just become normal to speak like that, so normal that most of the time you just can't see it, just another leaf dropping into the pool. So what needs to happen is for that pool to be cleaned out. To do this you will need to have those conversations that you have never had before, each of you being totally open about things that haven't worked or upsets that you have had and never addressed. This is of critical importance and without this the way forward will be blocked by these unspoken issues. Nothing can be built. Do not pass go, do not collect £100! When you have cleaned up the past- and this will be ongoing during your relationship not just a once only you've ticked the box exercise- then any conversations or incidents that arise that don't work for you or you partner will show up so much more clearly. As an example, if there is a communication or cross word that doesn't work for my wife or my family delivered by any of us, then it's as though a bomb has exploded in our house. When this happens it now shows up as so intolerably stark and obvious that we just have to deal with it immediately. Therefore, there is never any drama or upset. We have trained ourselves to be vigilant and not step over things that don't work.

15

Does this mean that we are not self- expressed and tread on eggshells around each other in case we cause upset? Well, no actually, the opposite is true. Anyone can speak about anything at any time without fear of it being badly received or fear of rocking the boat. I promise you that it is a glorious way of living and totally possible for you. How I know that it's possible is that if we created it like this so can you!

How do we start to have these conversations? Firstly, as a couple and for ourselves we need to get clear on the impact of living our lives like this. We then need to see how intolerable and divisive it would be if it carried on this way. You can begin to do this by sitting down with your partner and sharing from your heart how you would like things to change. However, there is a danger here. A human tendency is to go to blame whenever there is a problem. You may be saying 'well I don't do that' but trust me you do. It's just a defence mechanism that can work to defend us from the world but causes havoc in our lives. Here's a great way to overcome this natural tendency. Go to your partner with a gift. This gift is you being honest about your part in the relationship. If you are following this as a couple, then take it in turns to be honest about your individual responsibility. Don't point a finger in their direction but look at how you have been. This will open up a conversation instead of what often happens which is the blame being levelled at you/them has to be reacted to. You are then both stuck in being right and reacting to each other verses having a fruitful valuable conversation. Here are the suggested exercises that you can use to be in communication with a commitment to your relationship and being honest with each other.

Actions to take:

a) Sit down somewhere private where you won't be disturbed. This is so important for a number of reasons. Whenever you come up against difficult conversations the tendency will be to reach for a distraction and an interruption may occur as an opportunity, no matter how fleeting, for the thread of an important conversation to be lost.

b) Switch off your phones. There is nothing less engaging than talking to someone who is glancing at incoming messages. Again, the tendency may be to reach for your phone rather than speak about something that is occurring as confronting.

c) Don't do anything else when you are having this conversation. Give yourself totally to it. OK I'll allow a cup of tea or something stronger but not too strong and don't be eating a meal. I sometimes used to provide snacks for clients and then stopped when I saw them consistently reach for a nut or an olive whenever the conversation occurred to them as confronting. Anyway the no eating approach when having potentially difficult conversations leads to less indigestion!

d) Come to an agreement that you will both be civil and respectful in your communication. No raised voices or finger pointing.

e) One of you will go first and the agreement is that whoever is speaking is allowed to speak without interruption. The person speaking also agrees not to dominate the conversation by speaking for too long (you can make a rule for how long) and that they agree to bring up only one area at a time.

f) Now this next step may seem a little strange, but I promise you that it's essential for clear and open communication. When the person who is speaking has completed that particular conversation then the person listening repeats back exactly what the person has said without adding or subtracting anything. This can be a summary of what they have just heard- you don't have to remember every word said but it must contain all of the points. The person who is listening must then say, 'is that it?'

or 'is there anything that I haven't said or understood?' Or words that you are comfortable with but convey that you have been listening and that you now want to know if what you have heard was correct. I will expand on why this is so important in further material.

g) It may take several sessions to get everything aired but be patient.

OK so all of the above may take something. You probably have never spoken to each other so openly and it will require both of you to be alert to the others experience. It's not easy to hear someone levelling criticism at you and even harder if it's your partner. So, it's going to take something but what's harder, living a life time of frustration, guilt and dysfunction or spending a bit of time being honest with each other? I know which I would prefer. You are going to need to stop being right about your partner and about yourself, if, you really want a new more open and honest relationship. Now this may go a bit wrong to begin with as this is new and you may experience an adverse reaction to the process but stick with it and I promise you that you will reap the rewards.

Further Reading

When my wife Rachel and I first got together the decisions we both made to be with each other were slanted towards the practical. We had both recently come out of long-term relationships, Rachel's more long term than mine. I was very much impacted by separating from a relationship that I thought was for life and Rachel was facing a future as a sole parent with three young kids. I don't think either of us had seen each other as the perfect fit and even if we had been we weren't ready to see that because of our circumstances. Rachel says that she realised that she wanted me in her life when she saw me interacting with a session drummer's young child who came into the studio. She had thought 'that's who I want for my kids!' Romantic hey? My decision making was equally unromantic. I had wanted a family for years and had been in denial about that after being with partners who at the time weren't interested in starting a family and then me being 'oh well there you go, life's pretty good anyway', I saw being with Rachel as a whole new future. A future of family, getting away from London and a career that I had become disillusioned with, earning a wage working from a small country village. A whole new life. If I had a list of the perfect partner,

Rachel wouldn't at that time have featured on there and I wouldn't have featured on hers.

<u>Rachel's story:</u>

When I met Steve, I was at a low point in my life. I had recently separated from the father of my children after being together for 14 years. I didn't know where I was going to live with my kids. I met Steve when he signed the band I played in to his production company. He seemed like someone I could rely on. I saw him interacting with a young boy who was visiting the studio and knew that this was what I wanted for my children. He was a very nurturing person and I became attached very quickly. He gave me the confidence to sort out my moving house and listened to me talking about my concerns for hours. We decided pretty quickly that we would get married and have a baby. I had no idea that Steve was still not fully committed, although I did feel insecure and looking back, I was very much being a victim. I was suppressed in my interactions with him, generally letting him take the lead in decision making. When Steve returned from doing a course called the Landmark Forum, we got lots of things complete which we are now sure would have damaged our relationship over time. Over time the relationship became more equal as my confidence grew. We put regular communication into our lives and this has continued as the relationship has grown. Our relationship has now got to the place where how we communicate has an openness and honesty that simply doesn't allow for any conflicts to develop.

You would think that due to the process of our decision making that our relationship was doomed, wouldn't you? Well here we are 20 years later, four children, three grandchildren and a relationship that is totally solid and filled with romance and creativity. A relationship that we both, to be honest, never imagined. The reason that we have stayed together and grown our relationship is we believe due to using the techniques that I have presented in this book.

How we started our life together was pretty unequal. The kids were doing fine with Rachel, but I was clear that I could bring something to the table, and I loved being with them. I was also though, coming into the relationship thinking that I was a great guy for taking on Rachel's kids and even though I had asked Rachel to marry me there was no real long-term commitment in my thinking. I could be the kids friend and 'help out' but I wasn't prepared to go beyond that. Rachel therefore felt insecure and she later saw that she was being a victim and needy, which had me even more determined not to fully commit. Basically, I had left a back door open in our relationship so that I could escape if it got too tough. I'd also come from being a bachelor (all be it for a short spell) living in London, working in the music business to a rural village that actually felt like a suburban town with a plethora of net curtains, hairdressers and charity shops. Family life was also so foreign to me, with the focus being the kids welfare and little consideration for aesthetics and creativity and the order and quiet that I'd been used to. I compared the experience to David Bowie's character in 'The Man Who Fell To Earth', it all felt so strange to me. Also being with Rachel was very different from my last relationship. Rachel didn't wear make up, ate whole food and carrot sticks and everything in her life was about family. How I reacted to all of this was passive aggressively but often just nastily. I was often on Rachel's back about the place not being tidy and the children being unruly. Not that we didn't have fun and intimacy, we did but our relationship was unequal in the degree to which we had committed to each other and bound for failure or at the least dissatisfaction and unhappiness. Mostly my complaints would be made out of site but within earshot, 'howling at the moon', banging cupboard doors and lots of stomping. After about two years of this I did a course that changed my life called the Landmark Forum, where I saw the impact of me being this way with Rachel and the impact this could have on the kids. On the course I got to close that back door in our relationship and recommit to being the children's step dad and Rachel and I were able to create a whole new future together. I also saw the things that I was doing that were completely arrogant and I was determined to not alter. I used to, for instance, drive very fast on the motorway and Rachel used to sit white knuckled holding onto the passenger seat. I'd justify the speed I was going by saying that the kids got bored on journeys and it worked for the journey to be as short as possible, ignoring that we all arrived completely frazzled from a harrowing experience. I also used to believe that it was safer to stick to the fast lane and not have to lane jump. Of course, this resulted in me having to drive faster than everyone else in the fast lane but 'hey what can you do?' Another impact was that I drank every night at least a bottle of wine. Not great for the kids to witness, not great for my health and not great for Rachel as she has no attachment to alcohol. I justified this by thinking that my parents used to drink spirits which was much worse and 'it's just grape juice for God's sake!' I could go on as there is a whole very long list of things that I perpetrated on my family and friends and then justified away and hung onto without being present to the impact.

So what Rachel and I initially started creating was Chapter 1 of the program where we would take time to sit down away from any other commitments and really get in communication about everything to do with our lives together. We had both learned from completing the Landmark Forum that completion on your past is essential before moving forward and it wasn't easy at first as we both wanted to be right about our opinion of each other but after a short while we became skilled at communicating with each other so as to get to the hub of what wasn't working without making each other wrong. We would generally coincide these communications with going out for a drink or a meal. I think if you had been sitting within earshot you would have thought that we were on the verge of breaking up! I would say to Rachel 'OK how's life and our relationship going, let me have it straight' and she would outpour, then she would ask me, and I would speak. After I'd finished, I'd say, 'fancy another drink?' and we would effortlessly move on with life. It still amazes me that we can be that straight with each other and both be OK with that. We no longer have these meetings because we don't need to. If a cross word or angry interaction is ever unleashed in our home then, as I said earlier, it shows up so starkly that we are now compelled or more accurately, trained to deal with it immediately and then there is no or little impact. I'll use the analogy of the leaf falling into the pool again here, now the pool is clear of leaves (our undelivered communication, our making each other wrong, our justifications, our stuff) so that when one solitary leaf falls in (an argument, a crossword, a dishonest communication) we can see it immediately and deal with it.

It's now just become the way we live, it's natural, it's unexceptional, it's day to day and it works. What we then have is clarity and understanding so we can fill our lives with fun, joy, creativity and helping others less fortunate than ourselves.

It was once believed that the brain was developed in early childhood and then remained largely unchanged for life. In the later part of the 20th Century what was discovered was that in the first year of life the brain sheds vast amounts of neurons but also neurons can multiply throughout our life span. Simply put, our brains physically change due to our brains activity. Again, simply put, neuronal activity and multiplication of neurons through connection with other neurons arises out of those neurons being activated by use, -thoughts, habitual activity, motor activity etc- if those neurons aren't engaged then the connections won't be made. So if a habit of zero tolerance for unresolved conflict is practiced then after a while our brains will change and it will become natural to live and communicate like this. What we are aiming for here is a new way of being, thinking and acting that will produce positive results for your relationship and it's entirely possible!

Before writing this book, I did a lot of research into people talking and writing about creating better relationships. There are many

26

books out there, great books written by committed and knowledgeable people. There have also been extensive empirically executed research studies completed into couples, their lives and the way they communicate. What is generally presented looks at the symptoms and what can be done about alleviating them rather than getting to the source of what's going on. This can I'm sure cause positive results as people are then actively looking at their relationships but there is a danger of any results being short lived as people aren't getting to the source of what is really going on in their relationship. So, what do I mean by getting to the source? I know many people in my life who have persistent ill health that regularly interrupts the day to day running of their life. How they generally deal with this is by going to the doctor and taking medicines or by buying over the counter non-prescription medication. They may also decide that what they need is a healthier life style and look for ways to improve this. However, the symptoms generally persist as they never get to the source of what's really causing this ill health. Medication can do miraculous things but if the reason for having the illness, the real reason, isn't addressed then the danger is that the symptoms will persist and often get worse. The same is true in our relationships. We can look at how romance is missing, or how our interest are too divergent, or we don't spend enough time together and we can put things in place with a commitment to a better relationship but unless we get to the source of what's going on, then these actions will probably not succeed in us having a better relationship. I'm not suggesting that creating romance and fun and more time together isn't of value, it's just that without going through the process of Chapter 1 and its actions any improvements will be short lived. What I've attempted to avoid in this book is looking at the detail of conversations or communications and the detail of how we can create new conversations and communications. Why? Because I am committed that you get to the source of what is going on in your relationship and not get fascinated by the symptoms then conversations and actions will arise naturally.

I want to look at an example of what I'm referring to here. I've chosen this particular book because it has been critically acclaimed, and the authors come from a clinical background and have researched relationships over a long period. John M Gottman Ph.D. and Joan DeClaire write at length about how we communicate in their extensively researched book The Relationship Cure. They look at the process of bidding that we use in our daily life both in our relationships and in all relationships. Gottman discovered, from scientifically researching how couples interacted, that the key to harmonious and long-lasting partnership was not the quality or depth of our communications but the reciprocal too and froing of often seemingly mundane exchanges which he calls 'bids'. The authors then go on to create new ways to introduce effective 'bidding' and responding to 'bidding' into our relationships. Gottman worked with 60 married couples over many weekends, observing them interacting with each other whilst housed in a mock-up of a small studio apartment. He learned that couples either turn towards, turn against or away from bids and correlated these behaviours with the status of their relationships ten years later. The conclusion- very much summed up in brief here- of this extensive research was that the couples turning towards bids, talking and sharing details from their lives and being playful with each other were by far the most successful at creating long term solid partnerships. So, the focus of the first part of their book looks at how to be more adept at creating bidding and receiving bidding successfully. What I think that we are really looking at here however is the symptoms of relationships that are not working successfully. It has very little to do with the frequency or quality of these bids and of course there would be some benefit to learning what works and doesn't work but unless we get to the source of what isn't working in the relationship any progress will be short lived. I know of many relationships where the bidding process is very unsuccessful where one partner is intent on telling their stories and not really listening to their partner. These relationships have lasted for decades, so there is clearly something else that's sourcing this relationship and giving it longevity.

29

What I think is happening is this: The glue that binds these couples together is the context that they have created for their life together and the context is reliant on the commitment they have to each other. I will say more about this later when I look at the positive impact that creating a context for your relationship has in Chapter 3. However, are these relationships that have longevity happy, harmonious relationships? I've often experienced people relying on each other so much and having so much investment in each other and their lives so predicated by unconscious and destructive habits that they find it almost impossible to even imagine being apart. They then spend a lifetime avoiding saying what is really there for them about their relationship and their partner and live resigned to that it will always be this way.

I'm not going to suggest that you stay in a relationship that you are clear doesn't work for you. I know many people who have separated in a civil and productive manner and our now much happier in new relationships. However, the fact that you are reading this book leads me to believe that you are still committed to making your relationship work.

It's surprising that we have structures for the most important things in our life but for our relationships we drift through them in an abstract unstructured often chaotic way and expect them to work. Or maybe we don't even expect them to work but we carry on like this regardless. We also rarely get any instruction of how to proceed with intimate relationships to have them work. There's certainly no or very little formal education regarding relationships. How we learn about relationships is largely from experiencing our parent's interactions. This will be gathered consciously or without conscious awareness from experiencing our parent's interactions with each other and with ourselves both overtly and also very subtly. Learned behaviour can even be picked up prenatally in the womb. I'm a keen football fan and get great joy from the excitement of watching football live and on the TV. When my wife was pregnant with my son, she could feel him get excited when I was watching my team Liverpool on TV and at 18 years old he still has that excitable energy (although actually he hasn't got any interest in football!) I'm in danger here of jumping to conclusions based on a desire for a good story so forgive me. It's pretty clear however, that children who grow up inside of a dysfunctional family often go on to exhibit similar dysfunctional behaviour themselves in their future relationships and have unsuccessful relationships. Learning happens in many different ways: Observational Learning, Imprinting, acculturation, tangential, amongst many, many others. Benjamin Bloom a renowned American educational psychologist has suggested that there are three types of learning, although they aren't mutually exclusive of each other. These are:

Cognitive Learning: problem solving, analysing, recalling etc

Psycho motor Learning: dancing, swimming, driving etc

Affective Learning: worship, fear, love etc

These types of learning are often connected to create complete learning of a process or task. In playing football for instance you would need to be aware of the rules of the game through cognitive learning, you would also need to practice certain skills with the ball and developed how to run faster etc and then you may develop a love or even worship of football.

So, we come into our relationships with a limited understanding of how to be in a relationship and have it work and with all of the conditioning from these many areas of learning picked up from the environment that we have been exposed to. Most people also have a limited awareness of how to function in the world successfully for themselves let alone when they 'rub up' against other people's conditioning. It's no great wonder that a large number of relationships flounder. So, the answer or at least what has worked for me and my clients is to put in structures that will enable us to have some success in bypassing our conditioning. Albert Einstein said, 'No problem can be solved from the same level of consciousness that created it' Which is why we then need a new approach that provides something else, some new way of thinking and communicating. If we don't schedule time in to speak and have new ways of communicating, then we will be following the same old patterns of conditioned behaviour and get the same results. I've noticed in the past few years the amount of opinions I have about people who I don't know, know nothing about and are in my life for only a very brief moment. An extreme case of this is when driving. I've noticed that when I'm driving, I will have an opinion about people in the car coming towards me from the opposite direction. It can be based on the make or type of car that they are in, the colour of the car, the speed that they are going, the way that they are driving; are they swerving or steady, are they on a mobile phone and on and on. Summing them up in a moment. I've also noticed doing it with pedestrians, having a whole dialog about them and their probable lives. Try it out for yourselves, start noticing the opinions that you may have about people that you know nothing about. If this is happening with complete strangers, then what deeply entrenched opinions do we have about our partners? Notice the extent to which you will be observing them and then judging them. All of these opinions and judgments are rooted in the conditioning from the environment that we have been exposed to. So, something needs to shift to give our relationships a chance of success.

How do we bypass our conditioning? The way I approach this in this book is simply by following the exercises and not doing your own thing which generally hasn't been working. Then it's for you to begin being present to when you are being run by your opinions, fears, likes and dislikes etc. Repetition in not engaging with these thoughts will have you experience a freedom where you will be able to engage in new more empowering thoughts and actions.

35

●

Chapter 2

Effective Communication

Introduction

If you haven't yet read Chapter 1 then I strongly advise that you
to do so before going into action with Chapter 2. The reason for this is
that until you have both been honest with each other regarding your
past behaviour and interactions, any progress will be limited and almost
certainly unsustainable. Remember the pool analogy from Chapter 1? If
the chapter 1 actions have been completed and you are now ongoingly in
communication about what hasn't worked in your relationship then like
the leaf dropping into a clean pool, what doesn't work, either in the area
of conversations or actions, will show up clearly and can then be dealt
with. Remember though that Chapter 1 or in fact any of the different
actions that will be presented are not a 'do it once only and tick the box'
exercise but are to be used and integrated into how you communicate

for the rest of your time together. Chapter 2 is about creating real communication and ways of you **Really** understanding what is being communicated by your partner.

How To Communicate Effectively.

I'm sure that we have all experienced times when what we have said has been misconstrued and we have been baffled as to why that is 'surely they couldn't have got that from what I said, they just can't have been listening'. Those times when you have made it absolutely clear that you have 'really appreciated' a meal that they have cooked or the present that they have bought you or their new clothes etc or you have demonstrated that you love them over and over again and 'they just don't get it!'

Instead of us acknowledging that what we have communicated is at odds with how our partner has received our communication, what human beings generally jump to is that there is a problem over there with them and not here with me. Consider this, what you communicate comes directly from how you perceive your 'reality' and your partner receives your communication from how they perceive their 'reality'. There is no 'reality' as such but just how you both perceive the world around you. You 'hear the other' through one's own projected belief of what the other person is saying. This can then be a wildly inaccurate interpretation. In the further reading section, we will look more deeply into the theory of parataxic distortion but it's unnecessary to go deeper into this here but just to know that it's happening.

So now you have a problem! Your speaking is shaped by your interpretation of how the conversation will be perceived by your partner and formed by who your interpretation of your partner is, which, is created by your past relationships and experience and your partner is hearing you through their projected beliefs given by their past experience. This is how misunderstanding, mistrust and resentment is created in a relationship! It's rather like your communications have been put through a random word generator and spat out.

The above can occur as a bit conceptual which will not assist you in moving forward, so what I request that you do is to really look at how this relates to you and your partner. Think of an incident where, in your opinion, what you had said didn't land with your partner and there was then some confusion created. It doesn't have to be a significant incident but just one that demonstrates this misunderstanding.

I can think of a pretty trivial but perhaps illuminating example from my life that happened recently. My wife and I were traveling home in the car and talking about what to prepare for lunch. I suggested that because we had left over sweet tamarind sauce from last night's meal that we could have some soba noodles which I could prepare, and she could prepare some miso soup to have on the side. When we got home, I noticed that she was putting noodles into a pan of water instead of what I thought we had agreed which was her preparing the miso soup and me preparing the noodles. What we then realised was that she had thought that what I had suggested was that we have noodles with a miso broth and sweet sauce and that we prepare that dish together. Ok so far this is all, as I said, rather trivial, however let's look at it inside of the communication distortion I am talking about. My communication regarding lunch came from a) a desire to eat quickly because I was hungry b) to organise and get into action because I'm a natural leader and that's just what I do and if I don't communicate the actions clearly then they will be misunderstood.

When my wife seemingly started to do her own thing then I

immediately jumped to 'I'm not being listened to here' or, 'I'm not being trusted' mixed in with 'here she goes again just doing her own thing without any regard for my plans' Both of these thoughts and the subsequent communications were a result of my past which was then projected onto my wife's actions and communications . I can see clearly how my view of life and having to be the strong organiser was created and then how my not being understood was forged in early life. The way my wife heard the conversation was from a belief that she had to get it right because she thinks that she gets things wrong. This was then projected into the way she heard what I said which was forged from her past. The result was that we weren't listening to each other at all but just interpreting the conversation from our own concerns. We could go deeper into this misunderstanding because there will be many more distorted strands, but do you get the point? And this was just about lunch!

So where does this apply to your relationship? A radical suggestion here is that you could actually have some fun looking at these miscommunications. I'm not suggesting that you trivialise the big stuff that has really impacted your life together but looking at more trivial misunderstandings and getting to the source of why they happened can take the heat and significance out and you can then begin practicing being in each other's 'reality'.

So how we are communicating is not from how the conversation will be received by our partner but how we think that it **should** be received 'they really **should** know that I care for them and it's totally crazy that they don't because I've said it a thousand times!' It's going to take some shift in your position here as we humans love to be right and not take responsibility but the rewards of seeing communication from a different perspective are huge! The place to start is by you firstly both acknowledging that there has been a problem with your communication and then both of you taking on being fully responsible for how future conversations go and taking full responsibility for your relationship. Now maybe your partner isn't prepared to take full responsibility at this point and that may leave you with feeling that it's impossible to move forward but it will still be extremely effective if you alone declare yourself responsible. I know that with my marriage I have declared full responsibility for how it goes no matter what, even if I think that I'm right and that she is wrong then it's my responsibility to get it sorted. It's great that my wife has also declared this but even if she hadn't been prepared to then it wouldn't alter my commitment to the relationship. I just can't be the victim if I take this position.

The next thing to do is to start practicing with your communication, noticing how it is landing with them and noticing the triggers for you getting annoyed or frustrated and what triggers their adverse reaction from your communication. Try taking the **should** out of your opinion. There is no magic that will have this automatically happen. What is required is practice. We wouldn't expect to go and run a marathon without training for it and likewise it would be totally unrealistic to expect to suddenly change the way we communicate after a lifetime of it being another way. I'm asking you to be sensitive to how you communicate and how you listen to your partner. You don't have to suddenly make everything that you are saying wrong (what works here is to take on that there is no right or wrong but just what works and what doesn't) and you don't need to step over saying anything that needs to be said but just be more aware of the impact of your words and the impact in the way you hear what is being said.

I may be in danger of over egging the pudding here so I apologies, but I am really committed that you not just understand this but get it in your bones. Let me give you a fictional example to demonstrate how people often communicate and how that doesn't work for either of them. Let's call our couple Peter and Liz. Peter works in banking and describes his job as 'high powered, high pressure work in the city'. He also loves playing tennis which helps him relax and he does this twice a week. Liz and Peter have three children who are aged between 2 and 10 years old. Liz is a full-time mother and left her job in the financial sector when their first child was born. Peter leaves their home for work early at 7am and returns home at 7pm but this can often be much later. He is in time to put the eldest child to bed when he arrives home, but the other two children are already asleep. Liz's constant complaint is that she is exhausted from looking after the kids, cooking cleaning and generally running the home, she feels unappreciated and unsupported. She also feels that Peter doesn't really value her contribution and that he relates to the money he earns as his and puts no or little value on the work she does in looking after the children etc. Peter's complaint is that he works hard, brings in the money, is exhausted and comes home to a chaotic house and a disgruntled wife. They very rarely go out socially together and in fact they rarely ever talk much about anything together.

The way they generally communicate is with disgruntled jibes about the state of the house, the exhaustion that they both experience and how unfair it all is. They love each other but can't seem to make any difference to a relationship that clearly isn't working. Peter thinks that his wife should see how hard he works to provide for the family and can't understand when Liz says that he takes advantage of her and under appreciates her when 'she has it so good, not having to do the long commute and relentless hours and I come home and I'm as attentive and loving as I can be considering what I have to deal with'. Liz can't understand why he doesn't see how difficult it is for her and why he reacts every time she brings up the fact that she is exhausted. All her friends can see how 'unfair he is being with his not helping out and he has an escape in his tennis and it's just not fair!' He really **should** be more attentive and appreciative.

And who is right here? You can see that they are both stuck with their opinions of each other and their lives together. If Peter could see how it must be for Liz and Liz see how it must be for Peter then they could have open and meaningful conversations and, in the process, get some practical solutions for what they are dealing with. Instead they are stuck with a big **should** blocking the way in all of their interactions rather than with the question 'why?' or' how must it be?' for each other. What stops them is that they aren't looking into each other's possible experience but just focused on what they are personally dealing with. If they can take out the **should** and blame, then they have a fighting chance!

It's all pretty obvious and simple, isn't it? We make it all very complicated so that we don't actually have to do much about it!

Actions to take:

a) Complete reading and take the actions from Chapter 1 if you haven't already.

b) Revisit the actions from Chapter 1 to see if there are any more undelivered/unresolved communications. There will be!

c) Acknowledge to each other if you haven't already, that the way you have been communicating hasn't worked for your partner. Remember to take a gift which is you taking responsibility and not pointing a finger at them!

d) Have a conversation where you remove the **should** and really get into their world no matter how crazy and illogical you think that world is! Remember that it's not the way it shows up for you that's important here but the way it shows up for them. Be generous! Really speak from how it will land for them and get how it must have been in the past when they were misunderstood.

e) Now look to see if there has been any progress. You will know because you will have the experience of it all being lighter and less significant and see that it will be the same for your partner. It may all be a little turbulent to begin with so don't be concerned as it's usually this way when approaching something new, especially when you have had a lifetime of generally not being in another person's world.

f) Do the above over and over. It will then become just the way you communicate.

g) Get it all wrong and don't worry just try again!

h) If new complaints about past communication or incidents are uncovered then go and get them sorted by using Chapter 1 again.

I) Be on the 'look out' for you both wanting to 'point score' and be right. What's required for this to work is for you both to give up your stance and determination to win any disagreements.

Further Reading

I want here to look a little deeper into why real communication seems often difficult to achieve in our relationships. From my time spent working in recording studios as a record producer I started to see that how we perceive is given by our conscious and unconscious opinions and views and often little to do with the information received through our senses. I realised from my direct experience and study that it was very easy to start listening to the music being produced in a way that was divorced or partly divorced from how others might hear it. This could be with individual sounds or with the overall sound of the track. How this happens is fairly complex, but simply put, we have a tendency to 'fill in' on what we hear. This 'filling in' can occur from a desire for the sound we are using or piece of music that we are working on to be different than it actually is. We may be hearing it as warmer or fuller, bigger or clearer etc than others hear it. We are basically hearing what we desire to hear verses what is really there or at least may be perceived by others. This phenomenon can also occur unconsciously. The sound say of a snare drum can be a distortion of what is actually there because it reminds us of a similar sound that we have heard before and then there is a 'filling in'-an actual sonic construction created by our minds. There has been much research done to back up this theory and a label given to this perceptional illusion called the phonemic restoration effect where they have seen that sounds that were missing can be restored by the brain.

A similar filling in has been discovered from research done into visual perception. Allison Sekuler, associate professor of psychology at the University of Toronto researching this phenomena says "what many people don't realise is that the objects we see are not necessarily the same as the information that reaches our eyes so the brain needs to fill in those gaps of missing information." She went on to say that " people relied on contours that were not really there, but that had been constructed by their brains."

A similar 'filling in' occurs in our interactions with others and has been labelled as Parataxic Distortion, after research done by Harry S Sullivan, an American Neo-Freudian psychiatrist and psychoanalyst. He talks of a fantasy personality that is created from our past experiences, our view of the world and others. When that view is then contradicted by interactions with the person who we have imagined or constructed as being a certain way there is a phenomenon that we call cognitive dissonance which can cause stress. We then imprint or concoct further stories about that person that helps us cope with the stress of this cognitive dissonance. We can then lose the ability to be able to listen to the other person and listen through this Parataxic Distortion, not to what they are actually saying, but what we think that they are saying given by our conditioning. This process can actually be valuable to us when we are interacting with someone for the first time and for short periods as it acts as a short cut to begin communication but when we really believe that this initial view or short hand version of the person is who they are, then there is no access to really understanding them and little way of interacting with them in a productive way. We may also have a destructive habit of trying to fit the person into our view of how they 'should' be by manipulation and coercion. Take a look for yourself at how in your life you may have been surprised by a person's behaviour; they may have acted in an unpredictable way which has then altered your view of them.

I know that for myself I have often been surprised by the behaviour of someone that I thought I knew. When I say, I thought that I knew, I mean that I have summed up and concluded as being a certain way. For instance, with Rachel, my wife, when we first got together and for a considerable period after, I had an opinion about her that she was timid and often unclear in her communication. Basically, a bit of a push over (*I've made sure that she doesn't mind me saying this about her by the way!*) Now I know that sometimes she can be unclear and nervous with people, particularly when she is speaking to people that she doesn't know, this happens particularly on the phone but how I used to relate to her was from 'this is just the way she is, always'. Then I had an opinion that this was an aspect of her behaviour that I believed should and could be changed. Now I can see that the desire to change her was so that she could fit the picture of how I thought a person I was in a relationship with should be. There were lots of things about her that I loved but this wasn't one of them. The parataxic distortion I had created of her occurred to me as so real that it was a profound shock to me when I saw her being the opposite of this. I can still vividly recall the exact time and location that my new experience of her clashed with how I had perceived her up to this point. There had probably been other occasions when she was being like this, in fact I know now that there must have been many other occasions prior to this. We were in a London Hotel and it was at about 11pm and Rachel was sitting cross legged on the bed and talking to her brother on the phone. The way that she was speaking was so surprising because it didn't fit at all with my perception of how she should be speaking due to the image of her that I had created. Her speaking was so clear, insightful and powerful that it took my breath away and immediately my opinion of her altered. Up to that moment the way I communicated with her was through this parataxic distortion and I now realise that I wasn't really listening to her but listening through the opinions or views that I had created of her. Something then shifted in all of our communications. From that moment on I had a view of her as being clear and powerful in her communication and when she wasn't or isn't being that way then I'm now surprised! She isn't of course either of these ways as a personality or identity but just occasionally reverts to being one way or the other in certain situations. What's liberating and massively impactful for our relationship is that I now know that this distortion happens and now that I am aware of it, I can interrupt it and really get into her world verses writing her off. I can now see clearly when she occasionally isn't being clear and powerful in her communication and I can then support her with this. Not now from a desire to change her to fit how I think she should be but now with a commitment to be in real partnership with her.

●

CHAPTER 3

Commitment

Introduction

If you have already read and used Chapter 1 and 2 previously then thank you for engaging with it and thank you for continuing reading this. Chapter 3 is all about how the results that you have probably started to experience from the two previous Chapters can be integrated into your life in a sustainable way. As I have said previously these actions are not to be completed just once but are there to be used in your life ongoingly. You will experience over time that this new approach to communicating with your partner will become easier with use and after a while it will alter the way you live your lives together and this new way of communicating will just become normal and an effortless everyday experience. The Chapters can be approached after using them for the first time in a none linear way. You won't necessarily need to go back to Chapter 1 again and start going through all of the steps if some difficulty arises in your lives. This approach will become clearer as you start using the exercises. Please remember that there is no magic happening here, any results caused will be a function of you using the book and integrating it into your lives.

Commitment

If you have been using Chapter 1 and 2 then the fog of confusion and frustration that you may have been experiencing in your relationship should have started to lift and a new partnership will be forming. This Chapter looks at how to sustain any results that you have had and how to integrate it into your everyday life.

For those of you that are married or have a civil partnership, do you remember what you promised in your vows? You may have used the traditional vows of love, honour and obey but you will more than likely have written your own. What can happen and I'm sure generally does is that those vows are given some serious thought prior to the wedding but from the wedding day onwards we generally aren't present to our vows, save perhaps, for the occasional use of them in attempting to get one up in an argument! I've been with my partner for 21 years now and we were married 18 years ago. I have no idea what we promised to each other when we were married and can't say that I've given them a moment's thought since that wonderful day. I know that at the time I was so connected to my commitment to love and nurture my wife that the vows didn't seem important. They were just words. But how long is that promise really alive for us?

Vows aren't generally made within the context that they were created. A vow is an agreement between people or a promise or pledge but certainly how my wife and I saw our vows was more of an acknowledgment of each other that created a lovely feeling and brought us closer, not a binding agreement. When was the last time that you asked your partner how the vows were going for them or even asked how the relationship was going?

What I have witnessed is missing from relationships where communication has broken down is a stated commitment to each other. Literally a context for the relationship inside of which all conversations and actions take place.

So, what do I mean by this? Below is a great quote and although he is talking here about companies, I think relevant to relationships.

"There's a difference between a brand promise and a brand commitment. It's easy to promise. It's hard to commit." Greg Cordell, Chief Inspiration Officer, Brains on Fire

What I think Greg Cordell is getting at here is that it's easy to make a promise and to break that promise, 'I promise to give up smoking' is a common one that we have all heard and seen flounder or are often short lived, 'I promise that I will never do that again'. A commitment however is a call to action. The promise to give up smoking is much more powerful a statement and ultimately more sustainable inside of a commitment. If you state, 'I am committed to a long fit and healthy life', then smoking can't really exist inside of this commitment. Not that someone's smoking habit is going to magically disappear by stating this commitment but if it is linked to this bigger context for a healthy life then it will have a greater chance of success. So, what has this got to do with relationships? Let me give you an example from my life.

As I said earlier what really worked for my relationship is that my wife and I would schedule in time away from the family to talk about our relationship. We don't need to do that so often now, as we have these conversations ongoingly. We would go out together for a drink or a meal or just out walking together and if you had been a witness to our conversations, you would probably have thought that we were on the verge of breaking up, because we would speak openly with no holds barred. How the conversation used to go is that we would check in with each other how it was all going. Literally I would ask, or she would ask the question 'how's it all going?' then one of us would outpour about everything that was working and wasn't working about our partnership. We had already agreed how to manage these conversations and the structure that we thought would best work and they were completed because of our love for each other and our commitment to our marriage working for both of us. We were then inspired to restate or state anew our commitment to each other. So, let's say that we made a commitment to have a fun, safe, joyful and loving family home. Living inside of that commitment every conversation and action can be assessed. I know that I can't be rude and uncaring if I am living from that commitment and likewise for my partner. If a conversation isn't coming from that commitment, then it will show up starkly and then it can be dealt with.

Our relationships are often operating inside of an unstated and unrecognised commitment. If we were to be asked the question, 'are you truly committed to your relationship working', then the answer will almost certainly be, 'yes of course', for most relationships. However, if we were to look at how we are living within that relationship, how we are acting and what we are doing, we would probably see something else going on. How many of you know people who say they are committed to something but then their actions show the complete opposite? We may say that we are committed to being fit and healthy but then our actions are in no way correlated to this statement. We do very little exercise and eat unhealthy food. This also applies to our relationships. We say that we are committed to being in a caring loving, supportive relationship but what we are really committed to is being right about our views and dominating with those opinions. The best way to see how we are living in contradiction to our commitments is to really get the impact of how we have been operating and then recommit to our partners.

So how do we make this commitment, and have it present in our lives? The first thing to do -remembering that here you have already completed Chapters 1 & 2 - is to talk together and get creative. Really get in touch with what inspires both of you in your life together. Don't be too concerned about how to make it happen at the moment but be free to dream of the life that you both would love. If what comes up is resistance from either of you to this process, maybe some bitterness about 'how can we possibly have this', because of past behaviour, then go back to Chapter 1 and make sure that it's complete for both of you. Remember here that you're not looking at the actions that may be required but just creating a commitment to each other. Don't make it too complicated! It can be created with a few words, love, joy, fun, nurture. The pull will be to come up with something that is created from the restrictions of how the relationship has gone in the past. This will limit how you will see the future. This is now new, so as far as you can, create without a concern for what has happened in the relationship previously. The predictable state of a human being is to be resigned, saying, 'it can't possibly work because ......' or, 'you don't know my partner, they will never stick to anything' or, 'we are just too busy and exhausted to make time for this', or some version of these. If you want to keep the relationship the way it currently is then go ahead and be resigned, if you want something different, something inspiring, a relationship that you never dreamed was possible, then what is required is for you to give up your resistance and CREATE something new!

Now write it down as it will disappear from memory quicker than you created it. Put it somewhere visible so that you keep present to it daily. After a while you won't need to write it down to remind yourself, because, it will become simply the way you live your lives together. In my relationship with my wife, if one of us was being an arse for more than a moment or two, it would occur like the film Invasion Of The Body Snatchers where an alien presence has taken one of us over!

You may be asking at this point 'how is it going to be possible to sustain this'. Well again there is no magic that is suddenly going to change your relationship. It will require you being present to all of your communications and how you and your partner are acting and reacting in the relationship. You will make mistakes, you will probably get angry, it will probably occur like the relationship is worse at first because those communications and behaviours that before were just the way you communicated, will now be highly visible. Stick with it as the rewards are immense. It's going to require both of you to stop scoring points with tit for tat, 'I was right, you were wrong', position taking. Not easy but so possible. If you notice that you have 'fallen off the wagon' then clean up the mess with each other and re commit to your future. Everything can be resolved by openly and lovingly talking and listening.

What really works to keep the commitment alive is to schedule in time to sit and talk to each other about what is working and what's not working. Don't just think that a five-minute chat over breakfast or meeting each other by the front door conversation will sustain it. It almost certainly won't. What will work is weekly or two weekly scheduled dates, were you can sit down in a relaxed atmosphere and talk. Put agreements in place were you both decide the structure of these sessions. Agreements like, no raised voices, no rude interruptions, no point scoring, being civil at all times etc. Think about how the interactions may go wrong, what would trigger both of you and put in some agreement that will help with that situation. The mistake that I've seen happen with some couples is that they schedule the first month and get some benefit from it but then they let it slip and it can become forgotten. This part of the program is vital! Schedule in dates as far in advance as possible. You can always re schedule those dates if some other commitment comes up but put the dates in your diary immediately!

Actions to take:

a) Complete Chapters 1 and 2 of the Book. Don't skimp on this. It would be like washing greasy dishes in cold water with no detergent! What would be the point? It's going to take a little more time being rigorous with this, but it will pay dividends in the future.
b) Schedule an initial session to create your future together. Make sure that you do this and don't just look at some times to speak, not agree a time that works for both of you and put it off. Also don't defer to the

other partner to make this happen, make it happen yourself beyond any reasons for it not happening.

c) Be inventive without a concern for how this will work. Remember that the pull will be to refer to how it's been in the past and your reasons for how it's not going to work this time. Resignation is your enemy here! Really imagine how you would want your life with your partner to look in the future. Imagine a relationship that you would be proud of the world witnessing. Every time you get stopped with disempowering conversations about how it can never be this way, then start again. Remember that you are looking at your future now from a space of uncertainty, as it hasn't been working the way that you would want. So, it's really going to take something. Where to position yourself is that you have both engaged with this book and your relationship is now back on track or working better than you could have imagined. From that space place yourself in the future that you are now declaring will happen.

d) Schedule in time for future dates as far in advance as possible. It's like you painting yourself into a corner with your commitment to making it work. Don't skimp on this, as scheduling time in, is you declaring that you are now committed to making this work and this is now your new life together.

Further Reading

'Commitment is an act, not a word'. – Jean-Paul Sartre

Commitment as stated by social psychologists is the experience of being psychologically attached to something and intending it to continue. Commitment has been described as being, 'locked in', to something one wants to sustain, or cause, and although this may not be the most inspiring and empowering description of this commitment in action, it demonstrates the difference to perhaps just promising something to someone.

What arises out of a commitment is action but to commit or be committed to something is a declaration of intent to a future not in itself an action. The declaration can be made internally to yourself but is always more powerful when it is shared with another. To make a promise is different than making a commitment. The promise can come prior to a commitment or in tandem or after a commitment is declared. A promise is made and then there is a commitment to that promise being realised. In pioneering America, The Bureau Of Land Management allowed people to claim lands by putting a stake in the ground. Making a commitment to your relationship can be an ontological or vocalised stake in the ground. These pioneers didn't necessarily know how their lives would look on this piece of land. The land could often be barren and inhospitable, so, their futures were far from certain. Currently your future may look a little barren and uncertain but despite these circumstances a declared commitment to your relationship will give rise to a different way of communicating and acting in your relationship. Your commitment to your future together doesn't need to be influenced by your past or current circumstances or views. It can be created anew.

I'm sure that you have all heard of the statement 'throwing your hat over the wall'. There are several stories as to its origin. My favourite is the story about a group of school children who on their daily walk to school passed a walled garden and saw some apple trees tantalisingly peaking over the wall, that they could scrump from.

They were all scared about what might await them on the other side, so together, they made a pact that they would all throw their school hats over the wall , so that there would be no turning back from their commitment to taste the delicious fruit! In 1962 a large crowd gathered at the Rice stadium in Houston, Texas for a speech by J F Kennedy. The speech he gave that day was bold and audacious. He committed the government and therefore the people of America to reaching the moon before the decade was out. At that time the technology wasn't in place to achieve this result and the majority of Americans were against this idea. It was within this declaration- this throwing of the hat over the wall, that the required actions were taken to cause this result.

When this commitment is declared in a relationship, it's as if you are building a structure for the relationship to exist within. When a sports person makes a commitment, to say being first at what they do, or breaking their own personal record, their behaviour will clearly show up within that declaration of intent. If they aren't training sufficiently or have the wrong diet etc then that behaviour won't be consistent with their stated commitment, it will show up starkly and then be dealt with.

Let's explore a little more about what is available from committing. It's been statistically proven that couples that live together and later decide to marry are more likely to break up. There is a 33% higher rate of divorce than those who chose to wait until they were married before living together. Ok so don't panic if you are reading this and you are living together and deciding to get married! As you are reading this and in action with the steps it's a demonstration of your commitment to your partner and this will assist you in not being prone to the factors that lead to such breakups.

Let's look at what might be happening here with marriages breaking up/divorcing if the couple have been living together prior to the marriage. One factor could be that the marriage proposal was seen as a fix for a partnership experiencing difficulties. It could be that the couples say that they are committed to their partnership working, then see that it's not and then see marriage as a possible saviour, rather than marriage being a firm unconditional commitment to their future together. You can see how this might impact their future together. It could also be that there living together has come about through circumstance rather than any firm commitment. I know of quite a few couples who have started by spending weekends together, which, has then become weekends and a couple of days in the week and then 'well hell you're practically living here anyway so why not just move in'. Then marriage might occur as just the next step in that process rather than a firm commitment to be with each other. Dr John Curtis who is the author of Happily Unmarried states from studies he has carried out, that the difference between cohabiting men and cohabiting women is that women see moving in together as a stage towards marriage and men see it as a test drive for the relationship. You can see how these differing views may cause friction between couples.

Another interesting study showed that the hormone Vasopressin, which is a chemical released during sex, may play an important role in pair bonding. People shown with a higher level of this hormone were seen to be better communicators and were more committed to having their relationships work. Men who had longer vasopressin receptors were more likely to be married. Does this make us just slaves to our hormones? Well yes and no. If we know that our hormones are influencing how we are reacting to our partner and they are influential in deciding how committed we are to our relationship, then we can do something about it! A not too significant but relevant example of this was an experiment carried out in 1997 by Arthur Aron, were two people who had never met, were given a set of questions and an exercise carried out over a period of just 45 minutes. The 36 questions were designed to intimately delve into each other's worlds and then they were asked to stare into each other's eyes for 4 minutes. These pairs reported stronger feelings of intimacy than pairs who met for the same period and were not given questions. One pair even got married six months after the experiment! So, this proves little about the triumph of generated commitment over hormones but is an interesting example of intimacy being generated between two people. Another example of emotions being generated has been demonstrated by a small study carried out in 2006 by James Coan, at the University Of Virginia which, showed that if married women held their partners hand then there was a decreased brain response to threat whilst this wasn't the case for cohabiting couples. This may be why marriage is linked to physical health.

The benefits of couples committing to marriage rather than co habiting has also been demonstrated by James Coan. Coan has proposed that couples who have made a commitment to marriage had more trust for their partner. There was something about the experience of cohabitation were you *'are explicitly maintaining a little bit of distance. You're not locked in.'*

So where are you maintaining a little bit of distance? Perhaps you have a back door, as I did, from which to escape if the going gets tough. Consider that it's that back door that will almost certainly have your relationship flounder. The closing of that door by you and your partner, fully committing to your futures and how you will be with each other in that future will give you the relationship that you desire.

CHAPTER FOUR

Romance, Inspiration & Fun

Introduction

So, Valentine's Day what's that all about? One day a year where
we agree that we should be romantic. It's even for some of us expected.
As though not participating in it might be seen as some negative
statement about the status of our relationship. You can also look at it as
a lovely day when we get to acknowledge our love for our partner. Your
choice really. However, what it does I think demonstrate is an
acknowledgment that romance is important to us, even if just for one
day. I just want us to explore the world of romance for a moment.

Romance Inspiration And Fun

The romance I want to address- as this course is all about our relationships, is the romance created by two people to connect and bring a closeness to their relationship. Romance however doesn't have to be about or for another. People talk about the romance of Paris or Rome for instance. So romance can be about a place and it can also of course be about a way of being. People can be romantic in their approach to life or in their speaking and their tastes. One person's view of romance can also of course be diametrically opposed to another's. The Oxford English Dictionary's definition of romance is 'a feeling of excitement and mystery associated with love' This quote from Virginia Wolfe I find very romantic "Just in case you ever foolishly forget; I'm never not thinking of you". But to some it may occur as too understated or too obvious and lacking mystery and in fact romance. So, romance within a relationship has to connect with the other persons feelings, their likes and dislikes, their tastes really, to land as romantic. A romantic gesture can be as simple as a meal cooked for another. The requirement however would have to be that this was something out of the ordinary and not something the other person did day in and day out. The romance of Paris I'm sure would fade a little if one was living there for a prolonged period of time. So, the unexpected surprise of a gesture or word that

72

ignites a feeling of love or a feeling of desire, would be one useful way of defining romance. When was the last time that you ignited these feelings in your partner? What is it that would ignite these feelings?

When you were first with your partner, the experience was almost certainly that romance and intimacy came effortlessly. This would have been helped along by your body giving you large shots of dopamine and oxytocin which would have your head spinning, your heart racing and your rational thought process in tatters! People at this point in a relationship do unreasonable things, unreasonable as in without fully engaging their reasoning rational brain. To put it more kindly, they are driven by their passion and often blind commitment to their love for their partner. I remember with my first love, hitching hundreds of miles to surprise her at her place of work. Time, effort money etc etc were not considered, just an unstoppable drive to see this wonderful human being and to let her see how devoted I was to her.

I'm clear that some relationships have survived for many years without any romance being present. But at what cost to that full and complete experience of connectedness with each other? I know what romance provides for my relationship with my wife. It means that our love for each other instead of diminishing over time has grown. It also has our life together be exciting and fun. Now the problem for most of us humans is that we don't wake up into a romantic world. Life can often show up as rather prosaic and dull. So, romance needs to be created. You're going to need to use your noggin to get connected to how you could generate romance in your relationship! Really give it some thought. It's also going to require you to give up any resigned thoughts about how your partner is going to respond, or that it's really too late for all of this, or putting time considerations in the way, or tiredness or any other justification. Maybe for you it will be that tit for tat response of "well they are never romantic so why should I be" or, "they just aren't built that way", or maybe for you it's " they will think I'm foolish". Actually, discussing that romance is missing in your relationship and that you now want to create more romance would probably occur for your partner as romantic. You of course don't even need to call it romance. It could be talked about as bringing more fun, excitement and passion to your relationship.

Pretty much everyone will respond to romance, it's just that you have to get it from their perspective, to see what action or words will connect with them. I'm tempted to give a list of suggestions here, but it really isn't about that. It's whatever is going to work for you and your partner. It could be as simple as telling them that you love them if that is something that you rarely do, or it could be a surprise holiday to some exotic location. However, this isn't just a once only action but something that you can be doing regularly to bring that va va voom back into your relationship. To some people just listening and really understanding what they are dealing with can be romantic and even if you don't think that it is, then take it on board as it definitely won't do any harm to your relationship! Being romantic doesn't always mean that you need to be taking actions that you see as romantic. It can be how you're are consistently being in the relationship. When I look at my relationship, I can see that romance is weaved into the fabric of our relationship, rather than being something that would stand out from how we are generally being together. What I mean by that is that it has now become a habit that we do things for each other day in day out. We cook together, we go walking together, we play and listen to music and films together, we tell each other our dreams and fears. We also have dates together and go away on special weekends. All of this has happened from our commitment to each other and our relationship. If we weren't doing the above together then we would see immediately that something was up with us and it would be addressed. I think that the thing that is most romantic about my wife is that she is always looking out to support me and share my load and I know that she knows that I appreciate this and that I endeavour to be the same way with her. This didn't happen by some magic or because we are some kind of new breed wonderful human beings (although she is of course!) It was something that we created from getting into each other's world and finding out what made each other tick.

A complaint that generally arises (no pun intended) when relationships are not working or have become predictable and boring is that the couple have ceased to have sex together or rarely do. It's obvious if you are not communicating with each other, then this is going to impact you being intimate but also if romance is missing from life then that generally has an impact. If this is the case for you then I suggest that you go through the different chapters starting from Chapter one and be in communication about this. It can be an issue that brings up all sorts of insecurities and concerns. Sex can become a very serious, painful issue, loaded with meaning. However, it's just sex and has no intrinsic meaning and like most other things in life you can have fun with it and be creative and drop the significance. Remember how it probably was, for you both, when you first started out together? Well it can be that way again, if you are willing to bring some creativity and excitement back into it. Maybe if you haven't had intercourse for a while then agree with each other that you are going to just touch, talk and explore for a period of time without going all of the way. Light some candles, play some music, bathe together, massage each other with oil. I don't know! Whatever does it for you really but get in action and stop being right about your point of view because it's not working! The damage generally caused in our relationships often develops out of us not being in communication and being resigned about what is achievable. Get in communication and do it in a nurturing and respectful way. If you are worried or scared to do this then really look at the impact of not being in communication. Can you be with that? Remember how it may have been between you both at one time and rekindle that.

I want to look here in a little more detail what can happen when there is an imbalance in a relationship where one person has a greater desire or need for sex than the other. This can cause friction. If it's spoken about it can be a ' sensitive' subject and if it's not then it can be the 'elephant in the room'.

What may occur when addressing the subject of sex are various disempowering conversations that often come from our insecurity in the relationship.

These may be:

a) 'I want them to want me and not because I'm putting pressure on
them'.
b) 'If I talk about sex then it will take away from any spontaneity that we
could have in our relationship'.
c) 'It's embarrassing to talk about my needs.'
d) 'It really isn't that important to us. It was once but now I/we can do
without it.'

Look at how you may also use your partners lack of
engagement with sex to take on being a victim. There can be several
advantages to this position. You may have something going on around
rejection, something from the past that may be hidden to you or some
conversation that you aren't worthy of being loved. If your partner, then
'rejects' you by not intimately engaging with you, then this can confirm
the story you have about yourself. The opportunity that this then
provides is that you don't have to take responsibility for changing the
situation, you can dwell or indulge in these feelings of being rejected,
your needs not considered. This may sound like a crazy position to take!
Why would we want to do that? Generally, most human beings have
some insecurity around being loved. It's vital for our survival that we are

nurtured and cared for. No matter how secure our upbringing has been, we often hang on to the question 'do you love me?' Our bodies are hard wired to protect ourselves, literally we have a defence mechanism that looks for danger. This defence mechanism can sense that being the victim, however crazy this may sound, is a safer position than being vulnerable and open and responsible in our lives.

So, what to do if this is there for us? Well just being aware that this may be what's going on for us will provide something, as you then have a choice to go down that road or see that it's just a function of your past and not engage with it. You can then be in action, communicating with your partner what is really going on for you. Yes, it's going to take courage but the impact of not being in communication is I'm sure that you will agree is far worse.

Actions To Take

1. Put down your phone, close your computer and start to use your noggin about bringing romance back into your relationship!

2. I could give you a list here of romantic things that you could bring to

the relationship, however we all have different tastes and different needs. The important thing here is to really get into your partners world and explore what they might consider to be romantic. It could be as simple as making breakfast for them in the morning, sending a loving text message, buying flowers, a ticket to a football match (sorry that just something that would work for me!) You get the drift. Get creative and don't worry too much about failing. The fact that you have made an effort in this area will almost certainly be seen as a romantic gesture in itself.

3. If you are struggling with ideas on how to be romantic then there are lots of books, articles etc to assist you. One is Laura Corns 101 Nights Of Great Romance.

4. If sex has become an issue for you either because you don't have or rarely have intimacy with your partner anymore or you aren't satisfied with the way it's been going, then schedule time to have a conversation with them or take some action. The action could be a romantic gesture to open you both up to being intimate with each other. If you need to talk then open up to them from your heart, don't be strategic just be honest without making them wrong. Remember that they will probably be having similar conversations and may be reticent to speak.

Further Reading

When you stop and think about it, romance can be a very dangerous state to be in. If we look back at the history of man/women kind as a species we can see that we have always predominantly been predators but for thousands of years and still to this day, in some geographical locations, we have also been the prey. Romance floods our bodies with a cocktail of feel good hormones that inhibit our rational faculties and can leave us open and vulnerable to physical and mental danger. So why has nature created this powerful drive to connect intimately with another human being? The more attracted to another human being one becomes then the more feel good hormones such as dopamine are released. This increases attraction to just one individual then motivates the individual to form a bond to protect any offspring. There are obvious benefits for us as a species.

In 2005 Dr Helen Fisher Rutgers University, New Brunswick,

New Jersey, along with colleagues did experiments to determine what was happening in the brain whilst people focused on the person they loved. These experiments were conducted using an fMRI scanner, which, showed the areas of the brain that were active when individuals were shown photos of the person that they loved. One of the first areas that was observed as active was the right ventral tegmental area (VTA). This is a dopamine rich area of the brain and is part of the 'reward system'. This area had previously been studied and shown to be associated with pleasure, arousal, focused attention and motivation to acquire rewards (Fisher 2005) Fisher also discovered that love and romance can be addictive. Using an fMRI scanner, she saw the same areas of the brain light up when people were experiencing love that are activated when people are addicted to cocaine and other drugs. These lovers also showed brain activity in the caudate nucleus, an ancient brain region, that assists us in integrating thoughts and feelings. What the scans also revealed is that women showed an emotional response, while men's brain response showed links to sexual arousal.

Really the above could be under the heading passion or desire not romance. Passion is an innate desire to be with another person and usually be intimate with that person. It generally has a half-life like a drug, reducing its effect over the early course of a relationship. The hormonal response lessens, giving rise to more rational and often disempowering thoughts about your partner. Romance in the early period of a relationship is probably generally generated naturally without too much thought or consideration. It feels natural and is driven hormonally. Later in the relationship however romance will require a degree of thought and need to be generated. We are hard wired with looking for confirmation that we are appreciated and loved. Almost all relationships have a natural falling away of passion and It's essential as this happens that the message that we send out to our partners is one of love, compassion and support if we want the relationship to flourish.

There are many studies about the different stages that relationships go through. I'm not going to refer to them here for reasons of clarity. Simply put what generally happens after the first period of a relationship where we are innately drawn to intimacy and love for our partner, is a falling off of these often-overwhelming sensations. To live for long periods in this initial state would almost certainly be unbearable and certainly not sustainable. This initial stage of a relationship is fuelled by feel good hormones. The relationship can then be in danger as the excitement of that initial phase can dissipate into disappointment and feelings of flatness. However, the first phase of a relationship can then be replaced by a deeper love and commitment for our partner. The hormone that is generated here is oxytocin. Oxytocin is generally produced by the paraventricular nucleus of the hypothalamus and released into our system by the posterior pituitary gland. People who release more Oxytocin are generally happier and have more successful happier relationships. For women Oxytocin is generated in childbirth and when lactating as well as at other times. It assists the mother in bonding with their child. In men Oxytocin is released during orgasm as well as in other circumstances. Oxytocin is released for both men and women during intimate moments, hugging, kissing and orgasm. Its function is to cause bonding with another individual or group. In studies it has also shown that men when oxytocin is released into their system can even have a negative reaction to other females.

Oxytocin is innate and released at certain moments for all humans unless there is some biological malfunction. It can also be generated in a relationship. This brings us back to romance. A hug, a kiss a kind word or intimate contact can all trigger oxytocin to be released. The act of generating this release of Oxytocin will also then reinforce the bond with your partner and set off a loop where the action generates oxytocin and the release of oxytocin will generate more action. Bingo! This is why it is so important to bring romance to your life or increase romance in your life.

So, what happens when you are not feeling so romantic or even attracted to your partner? How humans generally tend to be is that circumstances dictate how we feel and then how we relate to the world. We generally don't look from the reverse perspective which is generating how we feel despite our circumstances. If we can then do this then our circumstances can be altered by how we are being rather than us being victims of circumstance.

Studies looking into this, looked at how smiling can bring on a chemical reaction. Dr Isha Gupta from IGEA Brain and Spine witnessed that smiling generated from nothing released Dopamine into our system which increases feelings of happiness. Serotonin was also released which is a stress reducing hormone. Surreally studies on people who had Botox injections that meant they were unable to frown, showed that they were happier on average than those who could frown! How crazy is that! So really what I'm saying here is that if you are committed to a relationship with someone and stuff is in the way of that happening then you have to 'fake it to make it!'

Here is an exercise that you can do to have you get reconnected to feelings of love and compassion for your partner. Sit somewhere

85

where you are not going to be disturbed. Close your eyes and get present to your breathing. Just be present to breathing in and breathing out. Don't engage with any thoughts just be with them, don't push them away. Now visualise your partner and open your heart to them. Generate love towards them from your heart. Imagine that there is a thread running from your heart to theirs.

This thread is sending and receiving love to and from them. Do this daily. Start with just five minutes and then increase the time gradually. You can also of course do this exercise with anyone in your life.

CHAPTER FIVE

Real Partnership

Introduction

Consider that as human beings we are hard wired for protection. It can literally be a matter of life or death that we successfully protect ourselves from impending danger. It's not necessary that this danger be real, it can be a perceived danger. Most of the time this perceived danger doesn't materialise as a real threat, but this doesn't seem to lessen the degree to which we are still on guard. Consider that as humans we are pretty much always looking to control a situation, or others, or that we are being controlled. You could say dominating or being dominated. There are many ways that this can occur and generally the person who has the strongest will to survive will end up being the dominant one in the relationship. What I mean by the strongest will to survive, is that, at points in their life they have developed strategies for coping in life due to their circumstances. If they have been brought up in a family where there is much anger and aggression then the strategy that they adopt will either be to fight back or to hide out. Either way this will show up in future life. This kind of behaviour is not always overtly obvious, as unconsciously we are led to disguise how we are operating or at the least we know that it's happening but it has become habitual or we think that its working well for us so we carry on regardless of the impact. If we aren't conscious of our behaviour then, as discussed before, it can have a detrimental effect on our relationship. This next chapter looks into this.

Creating Real Partnership

One of the frequent complaints that I encounter when working with couples is that one of them or, sometimes both of them, are very driven people and they find little or no time to be with their partners. We have developed into an almost totally, economy driven society where it has become increasingly difficult for couples to survive without both of them having to bring in an income, or one of them needing to work long hours to support the other. This can mean that there is little opportunity in the week for couples to connect in all but a superficial fleeting way. After a while this can lead to intimacy missing from the relationship and a resentment that it has to be this way. Couples rarely strike a balance where they both experience being appreciated for their contribution. The pull -and this is generally from the male side of the relationship but not of course exclusively-is to use the need to raise enough income to survive in two ways:

a) A complaint about how hard they must work which is used to dominate their partner and point score

b) A way of not having to fully engage with their partner and take responsibility for moving forward in the relationship.

The income generated can also be used to dominate and control either, by the physical holding on to the finances and then controlling how the money is spent or a psychological control by making their partner experience any money shared as being more like a charitable giving.

Many of us have this thirst for success, which is generally driven by a desire to prove or disprove something about ourselves. At one point in life and usually this occurs when people are very young, some incident happens where we will be confronted by something. It could be to an adult an innocuous statement or act but to the child it has a deep significant impact. I remember being very small, perhaps 8 years old, and hearing my mother with a group of friends discussing something to do with a maternity ward. I asked, 'what's a maternity ward', which was met with howls of laughter and my mother saying, 'well who's going to tell him?' No one did, they just carried on chuckling as I left the room feeling humiliated, confused and upset. The decision I made at the time is that I'd never embarrass myself like that again, if I didn't know something then I'd find out for myself or just carry on not knowing. I spent a lifetime not knowing some very basic facts which really impacted me. I would never ask if I didn't know the answer at school and consequently there were great gaps in my education. The upside of this was that I learned a lot of things by experimenting which has meant for instance that my guitar and cooking style are pretty unique! However, it has often been a barrier to how I function both personally and professionally.

The decision that you may have made from an incident in the past, could be the strengths that you now have, and use to great effect, but it could also have a downside in that you are letting that strength blindly run your life and consequently impact your relationship. Do you have the below complaints with regard to yourself and your partner? If not then maybe you have some other complaint or interpretation that drives you forward.

1) Why do they work so hard, be so driven and have little time for me and the children?

2) Why do I have to work so hard and they get to be at home with the children?

3) Why do they always complain about the hours I work yet enjoy the lifestyle that my hard work has created?

4) Can't they have more consideration for what I want instead of doing their own thing.

5) If we don't work hard now, then we will be in financial trouble later on.

6) The hard work I do brings rewards to the family so it's important.

What I've also often experienced is one person in the partnership dominating by doing their own thing. They will work the hours that they think they need to work and enjoy the leisure pursuits that they think they deserve with little or no regard for their partner. They are also often subconsciously trying to not be dominated by their partner. What results is a lack of understanding for their partner and very little communication. Its then highly unlikely that this relationship will survive, or if it does then no true partnership will be experienced.

How my partner and I have made it work, over many years, is that all activities are discussed openly and freely. These will include everything around finances and the home, work, projects and leisure. This may not work for you but what has worked for us, is that Rachel knows exactly any future work or leisure activity I have scheduled and exactly how our finances are working and vice versa. We have separate bank accounts as this is more convenient but we both know exactly how much we are spending and how much we can spend. Rachel can move money from one account to the other as we have complete trust in how OUR money is spent. I bring the majority of the money into the family but I'm able to do that because Rachel manages the home, does the lion's share of the food shopping, cooking, and looking after our grandchildren when that is necessary. What this provides for us is: partnership, a really close trusting bond and a stability. It's also a demonstration that we are equal providers. Now not everyone wants to be like this in their relationship but have a look at the opinions that you have about how your partner operates and then be creative in looking how it would work for you.

Another way of dominating in a relationship for those with children is point scoring and using the bringing up of the child or children to take a position and be fixed in being right about parenting. This can of course become very emotional and occur as complicated. Children can suffer dreadfully when this happens and although overtly, they may not know that they are being used as pawns in this tragic game, they will almost undoubtedly be being damaged in some way, experiencing uncertainty and feelings of being emotionally insecure. In studies it has been shown that parental conflict can adversely impact children as young as six months old. Studies (Harold, Aitkin & Sheldon 2007) indicate that exposure to parental conflict can manifest itself in children exhibiting antisocial behaviour and criminality, aggression, depression and anxiety as well as negatively impacting academic achievement.

For the majority of us as parents the bond with our children is so strong that we experience them as almost a part of us. Any pain they experience is also experienced by us. If we therefore wish to get at our partner then what better way than through our children. We can do this by influencing how our children may see our partner, being positional and 'right' about how to educate or discipline them, being right about how they should behave etc. The list is pretty much endless really. When it comes down to it, we would rather be right and make our partners wrong than be the loving, stable parent that our children need to flourish. This may sound a little harsh and generally in my experience, looking at how they are being is understandably resisted by parents because it's pretty ugly! However, look for yourself and be honest with yourself. Have you ever used the children to point score and be right about your opinion?

As I said previously, we would rather our physical body dies than our beliefs. This is what we are dealing with! People will die for a cause and be Ok with that. This is how we are wired to protect ourselves- as crazy as this might sound! - and if we can really see that, then we can see the lengths we might go to to be right.

So how do we interrupt this damaging behaviour? Again, there is no magic that will have that happen. What is required is for you to get present to the damage that this way of being is having or will have on your children, your partner and ultimately yourself. Is that what you are really committed to? If not then it's for you to take 100% responsibility, stop using your children for point scoring and proving that you are right. It will take something, it always takes something to admit how we have been behaving and it will really take something to change how you have been being.

Actions to take

1. Find some time when you won't be interrupted and a quiet space to sit.

2. Sit quietly and without making yourself wrong start to look at how you may have dominated your partner. It may be that you have undermined or belittled them during conversations. Or used money to dominate. You may have used sex for this purpose. You may have dominated by using your partners views of raising the children.

3. Ask your partner what their experience is of you and the impact of your behaviour.

4. Really look at the impact your behaviour has had on your partner, your children, you. Don't be afraid to get present to what people have to deal with when you are being like this. It doesn't mean that you are a bad person. It's just that this behaviour hasn't worked and that you have been blind to how it has been impacting the people in your life.

5. With your eyes closed. Imagine how the future would look without

you and/or your partner looking to dominate or not be dominated.

6. Sit down with your partner and apologies. Remember to take a gift of you taking responsibility with how it has been to the conversation. They will almost certainly open up to how they have been that hasn't worked.

CHAPTER SIX

Conclusion

Introduction

Why are relationships often so complicated? In 2011, it was estimated that 42% of all marriages ended in divorce. That's a lot of heartache and upset and that's just the people who actually go through the process of divorce, not the people who separate without divorcing. I'm sure that we all have our opinions about why relationships can be so difficult, but it doesn't make much difference in having them work! Actually, it's how we are in a relationship that has us experience relationships as difficult, relationships in themselves are not difficult. To give us some possibly new understanding into our relationships I want here to look at how physiologically our bodies respond in an intimate relationship.

Conclusion

The reason I am introducing this inquiry at this point is twofold. Firstly, my commitment is that we understand how our bodies respond to being in a relationship so that we can experience some freedom in dealing with emotions and sensations that arise by understanding that these feelings are experienced by pretty much everyone on planet earth and most of them are just automatic. Secondly, I have introduced this subject at a later stage because it can be a diversion from us getting in action and shifting what hasn't been working. You will after this Chapter 6 have the opportunity of going back through the previous Chapters with a new understanding of what is happening between you and your partner. A caveat here, I am not a neuroscientist and my explanations of how the brain responds comes from a basic knowledge of the brain and I will therefore be using more general descriptions, so that we don't get lost in detail.

Imagine that you are sitting next to your partner and you have just had an argument. You are both angry and both know without a doubt that you are right. In this moment the physiological response is identical to the response you would have if you were being physically threatened. The reaction that you have to anger is identical to the reaction to fear. A threat is perceived by and processed by the amygdala. The amygdala is part of a very complex area of the brain called the Limbic System, which broadly deals with our emotional life and the formation of memories. The amygdala is a small but massively powerful almond shaped nuclei which picks up the threat of danger in being made wrong and kicks in with a response that releases Epinephrine, a chemical that is produced by the adrenal gland. This then raises your blood pressure and heart rate, sending an increased blood flow to your brain and muscles, you will at this point probably also start sweating. There are other chemicals released into your body but let's not concern ourselves with them now. You will then be triggered into fight or flight mode. Some of us will want to escape from the confrontation and others will want to dig in and fight our corner. Some of us will also freeze and our minds become a total blank. As the chemicals start to take effect you will probably start to talk louder and faster, changing your facial expressions to give out a warning that something bad is happening. When in the grip of this response, it is incredibly difficult to calm the nervous system. When our bodies sense danger, parts of our cognitive rational brain are shut down or dampened and the saved energy is sent via our autonomic system to parts of the body that will increase its effectiveness in protecting us from this perceived threat.

So why is an argument with our partner, someone we may love and cherish, perceived as a threat which then can trigger anger and fear? Our bodies are incredible organisms that have become hugely effective over 10 of thousands of years in detecting danger. We are constantly predicting the near and far future to scan for danger. As we go through our day, our unconscious, autonomic system is responsible for 95% of our brain activity. How we predict the future is from our past experiences and understanding. If something in the past has impacted us, then in the future there will be an automatic response if that event happens again. However, it may not be a rationally recognisable incident but could be a smell or a sensation or something someone says that is a subconscious reminder of some past incident. If in the past you have made a decision that people are cruel, from an incident that may have happened, then when your partner says something you now also perceive as cruel, the same sensations will be experienced and your body will automatically take over, the amygdala will kick in and you will be consumed by the chemicals released for your protection. In Luke Reinhart's 'Book Of Est' an account of being in the incredible EST training, he writes that the leader said that people would sooner their bodies die than their beliefs. That's why people will give their life to save someone else or give their life for a cause rather than having their beliefs die. This is what you are dealing with! The hold that our beliefs and opinions have over us is incredibly powerful. The subconscious mind is always going to initially triumph. Paul Hedderman in his talks about non duality says that the subconscious is always the fastest draw. It's always going to react first. The only way that we can triumph over it is to see it arising, get that it's just our humanity, that it's is our bodies way of protecting us, not make it wrong and then take action to divert it rather than let it control us and trash our relationship! So how is this even possible to control? I want to get into that a little later but for the moment I want you to understand, that this is how we are functioning physiologically and start to see how you get reactivated. What are the triggers and then what are the emotions and sensations you experience when in the grip of your bodies reaction to a threat?

What has assisted me in my relationship and life generally is relating to myself as an organism that has been input with data. This then helps me by taking some of the negative significance out of my experience of life and particularly in my communications. If I can relate to my responses as just dealing with the stored data, then it's a whole lot better than when I read into my response some significant meaning. When you think about it, what choice have we really had regarding who we are? If we were born to different parents in a different culture our personalities would be completely different than they are now. We would probably have different tastes in food, music, culture, different beliefs and a different moral code. We would be completely unrecognisable to who we are now. But how we relate to our beliefs and opinions is that they are ours and they are right. A construct has been assembled and then we relate to it as 'I', I am this and I am that, I like this and I don't like that, then we have strategies to repel all borders. That's how we are functioning in our relationships and that is why so many relationships fail! You don't have to like everything about your partner, you can have very dissimilar likes and dislikes as long as you don't relate to their likes and dislikes as a threat or somehow see them as disrespectful to our own beliefs, likes and opinions. Two of my dearest friends are in a long-term loving marriage, the epitome of a successful relationship. She is staunchly religious, doesn't swear and doesn't drink, he is very much an atheist and is very fond of drinking and can be a bit of a potty mouth. He has been a committed vegetarian for the majority of his life whilst she eats almost nothing but meat and potatoes and hates almost all vegetables. They have two wonderful children who are now very well-adjusted adults. Their relationship works because they don't relate to each other's contrary views on life and tastes as a threat! They respect each other's opinions and love and care for each other.

So here I want to look at the physiological response individuals have when embarking on a new relationship and then look at the pitfalls that can arise as the relationship progresses. Love is a wonderful thing! Setting our hearts to flutter and rendering our rational brain impotent. It can be an exhilarating and scary feeling, lovely when it happens and often very sad if it disappears. It can also wreak havoc on a relationship! Studies by Helen Fisher at Rutgers University, New Jersey proposed that there were three stages to a relationship's development. The initial phase is Lust. Men's bodies at this point release Testosterone and women Estrogen. This is followed by the phase of Attraction which gives rise to specific chemicals or hormones, these are, Dopamine which gives you drive to pursue your partner and is responsible for goal directed behaviour, Norepinerphrine, which puts your body in an alert state with a surge of energy and speeds up your heart rate. Serotonin can also be released at this stage, but this is more likely for women and it can actually decrease for men. Serotonin can divert the mind to think about your partner. The third stage or phase can occur after about 4 years by which time Dopamine decreases and attraction decreases with it. This phase is called Attachment. With attachment the hormones oxytocin and vasopressin are released having us create the desire to bond and nurture our partner. Oxytocin is also released when achieving orgasm and also during childbirth and breastfeeding and is thought to be responsible for bringing couples closer together but can also make you experience being needy and jealous. Vasopressin is released after sex and stimulates protective behaviour, it can also stimulate less negative communication, relationship maintenance, attachment security, support for your partner and more. This is what is generally occurring during the course of a relationship. The phases of lust, attraction and attachment can vary in length and can occur for shorter periods of time at any time during a relationship but generally they occur in this order and these hormones are released and effect all of us in similar ways.

This could all be perceived as not a very romantic and spontaneous reaction to another human being, but for me, knowing that my body is responding in this way helps me not give negative meaning to these sensations when they arise and gives me an opportunity to play and create situations that will stimulate these hormones. Our cognitive mind can be incredibly powerful, and we can use it to in a sense fool our unconscious mind. It has been shown for instance that when we smile as a reaction to stimulus it can have a beneficial effect on our physiology but as we touched on earlier, we also know that generating smiling when we don't even feel like smiling can also have a beneficial effect. Smiling uses facial muscles and when these muscles are used our limbic system is fooled into thinking 'hey there's a party going on up there' and goes into action releasing the feel-good neurotransmitters dopamine,

106

endorphins and serotonin. We can use the same sort of tricks with our relationship by bringing romance to the forefront, listening attentively, by saying 'I love you' more often, by acts of kindness and love, by generating passion etc. We don't have to be dictated to by our hormonal response or lack of response. There is much information out there that has views-some scientifically gleaned, about how to choose the perfect mate and what specific circumstances need to arise for us to have lasting relationships, how wealth or lack of, can affect our relationships, how in-laws can be detrimental, how the birth of children can effect a relationship. Most of this information is presented as factual. It's not it's just a particular view as is mine! We can have any relationship that we choose! We don't have to be dictated to by our circumstances, we don't have to be a victim of our circumstances! Don't wait for your relationship to work out but make it work out! Get in action. Go back over the chapters when there is something in the way of you both experiencing it as working. Stop listening to those negative thoughts. How do you do that? Well what you do is literally stop listening to your endless internal thoughts. If you don't interact with them then they won't grow, their hold on you will become weaker and you will experience more joy and freedom in your relationship and generally in your life.

Thank you for reading this book and I hope beyond hope that it has been of value to you.

Remember that although I am committed that you get immediate value from using this book, it may also take time to shift some of the habitual behaviour that has developed over time, that now negatively impacts your relationship. Stick with it and remember that resignation and cynicism are your enemy! Please be in contact as your feedback will be very valuable to me.

stevelovellcoach@gmail.com

Website: https://stevelovellcoach.com/

Notes:

Notes:

Notes:

Notes:

Notes:

Printed in Great Britain
by Amazon